21 Days of Life

A Devotional

Muhsin Thornton

Minute with Muh, Inc.

Philadelphia, PA

ISBN-13: 978-0692092880
ISBN-10: 0692092889
Library of Congress Cataloging-in-Publication Date is available.

Project Specialist, Barlow Enterprises, LLC

Legal Disclaimer
While none of the stories in this book are fabricated, some of the names and details may have been changed to protect the privacy of the individuals mentioned. Although the author and publisher have made every effort to ensure that the information in this book was correct at press time, the author and publisher do not assume and hereby disclaim any liability to any party for any loss, damage, or disruption caused by errors or omissions, whether such errors or omissions result from negligence, accident, or any other cause.

Ordering Information
21 Days of Life may be purchased in large quantities at a discount for educational, business, or sales promotional use. For information email:

Request Minister Muhsin Thornton to Speak
Email: minutewithmuh@gmail.com

But seek first the kingdom of God and his righteousness, and all these things will be added to you.

Matthew 6:33

"Whatever you focus on will manifest."

~ Pastor Steve Martin

Contents

Dedication

I dedicate this book to my beautiful wife. You made me love life again. You taught me to realize that if people don't love me for me, that it is their loss.

You taught me to be a better son to my mother, a better father to my children, and a better husband to you.

Most of all, you helped me rekindle my relationship with God and pushed me to go after my dreams no matter what.

I am forever indebted to God for the gift He gave me in you.

For these reasons, this book is dedicated to you -- my homie, my lover, my friend, my around-the-way-girl, my LIFE!

I love you,

Muhsin

Introduction

Welcome to *21 Days of Life*!

LIFE stands for Lifted Up, Inspired, Faithful, and Encouraged!

21 Days of Life developed from my live, weekly social media show, *Minute with Muh*, which are minute-long motivational videos that I post on my Facebook Page. The videos are extremely well received, and hosts of people reach out to me daily, both publicly and in private messages, to tell me how inspired they are by the show.

I asked God, "How can I make more of an impact?" He told me to turn *Minute with Muh* into a devotional book. God reminded me that it takes 21 days to change a habit. So, my hope is that everyone who reads this 21-day devotional is inspired and motivated every day of their lives.

To benefit most from *21 Days of Life*, simply read one devotional to start your day. I intentionally did not add dates to the pages so that you can start and stop wherever you choose in the book.

21 Days of Life is for Christians and non-Christians. It is for the young and the old. It is for anyone who is struggling through the issues of life. Trouble will always be in this world. It is what we do about those troubles that makes the difference in our lives. Will you choose to let life's challenges weigh you down or will you stay positive? Stay positive! Know that God will deliver you.

I want this book to motivate you to keep a smile on your face no matter what you are going through. I want this book to help you to stay positive about life. I want this book to impact your life like it's never been impacted before.

I want you to be Lifted Up, Inspired, Faithful, and Encouraged. I want you to enjoy LIFE!

MUHSIN THORNTON

God Has A Plan For You

Devotion 1

MUHSIN THORNTON

God Has A Plan For You

For I know the plans I have for you, declares the Lord, plans to prosper you and not to harm you, plans to give you hope and a future.

Jeremiah 29:11

�֍

Don't give up! There are reasons for you not to give up. There are reasons for you not to quit. Despite how terribly difficult your life may seem right now you are reading these words in this devotional, at this precise moment in time, for a reason.

God has a plan for you.

God knows that you are going to face obstacles as you journey through life, but He will strengthen you so that you can overcome those obstacles. I often see people frustrated because their plan is not working like the next person's plan. It's not supposed to! Although we are all made in God's image (Gen. 1:27), we are all unique (Romans 12:6-8). We each must follow different blueprints to realize the successes that God has prepared for us before the foundation of this world (Jeremiah 1:5). Yes, God's plan for you is already prepared. He doesn't want you to detour when there's a roadblock. He wants you to keep living. Don't stop, don't park, don't shift your life into neutral. Stay in drive and keep moving forward.

I don't care how rocky or bumpy life's road might get. Just keep moving forward. You will lose some things along the way. You will lose some people along the way. You will gain some enemies along the way. And trust me, you will even gain a few grey hairs along the way. Nonetheless, remember that *all* things work together for the good of those who love the Lord (Romans:28)!

LIFE Meditation

Devotion 1

God Has a Plan for You

Let's Meditate on Jeremiah 29:11

For I know the plans I have for you, declares the Lord, plans to prosper you and not to harm you, plans to give you hope and a future.

❄

What do you hear God saying to you today? So that you can remember, let's write what you are thinking and feeling down right now.

_____

_____

_____

_____

_____

_____

_____

Prayer Changes Things

Devotion 2

Prayer Changes Things

For the weapons of our warfare are not of the flesh but have divine power to destroy strongholds. We destroy arguments and every lofty opinion raised against the knowledge of God and take every thought captive to obey Christ.

2 Corinthians 10: 3-5

✄

Recently my wife was having an issue on her job. She told me it felt like her supervisor was singling her out. He was constantly agitating her, pushing work that was not my wife's responsibility onto her, making rude remarks, and even talking about her to the other workers. It got so bad that she began to cry and wanted to take the rest of the week off.

She just could not understand why this supervisor was giving her such a hard way to go. She does all her task in a timely manner and never receives complaints from her superiors, her co-workers or the people she serves.

I had three words for her: It's the devil.

The enemy does not want to see you happy. He does not want you to be blessed. He wants to see you miserable. He comes to steal your joy, kill your hopes, and destroy your life. We must recognize satan for who he is and for how he operates, and, in this situation, he was working through my wife's supervisor. I said, "Honey, it's time to go to war." We began to pray, tear down strongholds, and speak peace over the situation.

The next day my wife came home and said she had been written up. She was distraught about the write up. I comforted her and explained that wars are a series of battles that take place and that to win the war you can't quit when it seems that you have lost a battle.

The Lord reminded me of Daniel. In Daniel chapter 10, Daniel thought that God either didn't hear his prayer or that God simply was not answering his prayers. The angel of the Lord came to Daniel and told him to relax because there were angels fighting for him in the spiritual realm. The angel assured Daniel that his prayers were heard on the very first day and that the manifestation of what he was asking God for was on the way.

We kept praying and we began to fast too. The day after my wife was written up it was thrown out *and* the supervisor that wrote her up was disciplined. God truly is a rewarder of those who diligently seek His face!

Don't quit, faint, or give up after the first battle. Keep firing up those prayers. Your victory is at hand.

LIFE Meditation

Devotion 2

Prayer Changes Things

Let's Meditate on 2 Corinthians 10: 3-5

For the weapons of our warfare are not of the flesh but have divine power to destroy strongholds. We destroy arguments and every lofty opinion raised against the knowledge of God and take every thought captive to obey Christ.

❋

What do you hear God saying to you today? So that you can remember, let's write what you are thinking and feeling down right now.

_____

_____

_____

_____

_____

_____

_____
_____
_____
_____
_____
_____
_____
_____
_____
_____
_____
_____
_____
_____
_____
_____
_____
_____
_____
_____
_____
_____
_____
_____
_____
_____

MUHSIN THORNTON

Command Peace

Devotion 3

MUHSIN THORNTON

Command Peace

Then He arose and rebuked the wind, and said to the sea, "Peace, be still!" And the wind ceased and there was a great calm.

Mark 4:39

Have you ever felt like all hell was breaking loose in your life? Imagine it -- you lose your job, your rent is past due, your spouse is acting crazy, your kids are out of control, even your dog has an attitude.

If you want peace in your life, you must command it.

The Bible says the enemy goes around seeking whom he can devour. He's a bully and bullies look for the people who are scared and who won't take action or speak up.

The Bible tells us there was a great storm while Jesus and the disciples were on the ship. The disciples were very afraid. Jesus woke up and came to the top of the ship and he commanded the winds and the waves to stop. He commanded peace and stillness. Jesus took action. Jesus activated His authority. Today, you must wake up. You must act. You must activate your authority and command peace and stillness to your life's storm.

You have the authority to change situations. Don't keep sitting there and allowing the storm to overtake you.

Command peace.

LIFE Meditation

Devotion 3

Command Peace

Let's Meditate on Mark 4:39

Then He arose and rebuked the wind, and said to the sea, "Peace, be still!" And the wind ceased and there was a great calm.

✄

What do you hear God saying to you today? So that you can remember, let's write what you are thinking and feeling down right now.

_____

_____

_____

_____

_____

_____

_____

_____

_____

_____

_____

_____

_____

_____

_____

_____

_____

_____

_____

_____

_____

_____

_____

_____

_____

_____

_____

_____

_____

_____

_____

Get Up

Devotion 4

MUHSIN THORNTON

Get Up

Good people might fall again and again, but they always get up. It is the wicked who are defeated by their troubles.

Proverbs 24:16

❧

I constantly see good people *going through it* on social media. I mean these people are suffering through foreclosures, divorces, courts cases, and more.

At some phase of life, we all enter those times in which we feel as if we face trial after trial. However, this should not surprise us at all. In John 16:33, the scriptures warn us in clear and certain terms, that we will face troubles in this world. There is going to be a time when you get knocked down. The question is, what is your reaction going to be? You may be down even as you are reading this. You may be telling yourself, "There is no way that I can bounce back from this!" Listen to me, yes, there is a way that you can bounce back!

The Good Book says good people fall, but they always get up. Think about this -- you're reading this passage today. That alone means that God gave you a second chance to pick yourself up and try again. I've been through divorce and remarriage. I had a house in foreclosure, but four years later, I was able to buy another house. Why? I was able to turn things around because I decided to bounce back.

When we are going through life's trials, all we want to hear is that everything is going to be okay. My mom was so tired of hearing me whine and have pity on myself that she finally said to me, "Muhsin you are a man of faith and a man of God. You have kids that need you. Now is not the time to stay down". My mother was correct. Staying down doesn't get you anywhere. Feeling sorry for yourself, asking why they did this to you, and why they did that to you, doesn't get you anywhere. It happened. Now, get up. You are going to be okay.

The story of the prodigal son goes like this. There was a rich man who gave his two sons their inheritances. One of the sons went out and spent all that he had and ended up "down" in a pig pin. Then he came to himself, *got up*, and went back home.

Today is your day. Come to yourself and get up!

LIFE Meditation

Devotion

Get Up

Let's Meditate on Proverbs 24:16

Good people might fall again and again, but they always get up. It is the wicked who are defeated by their troubles.

�֎

What do you hear God saying to you today? So that you can remember, let's write what you are thinking and feeling down right now.

_____

_____

_____

_____

_____

_____

Your Biggest Cheerleader

Devotion 5

MUHSIN THORNTON

Your Biggest Cheerleader

And all the wall was joined together to half its height, for the people had a mind to work.

Nehemiah 4:5

Only you and God can truly promote His vision for your life. God is the One who downloaded the vision inside of you (Gen 15:1). So, I don't care if there's nobody that believes in your vision. You must believe. You must be your biggest cheerleader, you must be your biggest encourager, and you must trust God when everybody thinks that you're crazy.

People doubted Nehemiah when he started rebuilding the wall (Nehemiah 4:1). Despite their doubts, God downloaded something to Nehemiah and he encouraged and enabled him to do it. You must keep moving forward if you are to realize your vision despite what people are saying. Even when the odds are against you -- go get it. There's a reason God gave you a vision and it is not for you to sit dormant because you're concerned about who's not supporting you or who's not validating you. God validated you and God validated your vision. You're worried about who's not making time for your vision. Why? People make time for what they want to make time for; so, you need to start making time for your vision, because I promise you, they won't. Learn to give yourself a V-I-C-T-O-R-Y, even when no one else does.

LIFE Meditation

Devotion 5

Your Biggest Cheerleader

Let's Meditate on Nehemiah 4:1-5

Now when Sanballat heard that we were building the wall, he was angry and greatly enraged, and he jeered at the Jews. And he said in the presence of his brothers and of the army of Samaria, "What are these feeble Jews doing? Will they restore it for themselves? Will they sacrifice? Will they finish up in a day? Will they revive the stones out of the heaps of rubbish, and burned ones at that?" Tobiah the Ammonite was beside him, and he said, "Yes, what they are building — if a fox goes up on it he will break down their stone wall!" Hear, O our God, for we are despised. Turn back their taunt on their own heads and give them up to be plundered in a land where they are captives. Do not cover their guilt and let not their sin be blotted out from your sight, for they have provoked you to anger in the presence of the builders. So, we built the wall. And all the wall was joined together to half its height, for the people had a mind to work.

✖

What do you hear God saying to you today? So that you can remember, let's write what you are thinking and feeling down right now.

_____

_____

_____

_____

_____

_____

_____

_____

_____

_____

_____

_____

_____

_____

_____

_____

_____

_____

_____

_____

_____

Stay Strong in The Faith

Devotion 6

MUHSIN THORNTON

Stay Strong in the Faith

Then the Lord said to satan, "Have you considered My servant Job, that there is none like him on the earth, a blameless and upright man, one who fears God and shuns evil?"

Job 1:8

Then Job arose, tore his robe, and shaved his head; and he fell to the ground and worshiped. And he said: "Naked I came from my mother's womb, and naked shall I return there. The Lord gave, and the Lord has taken away; Blessed be the name of the Lord."

Job 1:20

Sometimes in life things just happen due to no fault of our own. I remember reading about the time that Jesus and his disciples came to a blind man. The disciples asked Jesus, "Who sinned, this man or his parents?" Jesus rebuked them and explained that neither the man nor his parents sinned but that he was blind, so the glory of God can be shown through his life.

It must be rough to endure trials and test and difficult situations of various sorts and to have people think that you are being tested because you've been living in sin or because you are paying for wrongdoings from your past. Stay strong in the faith. Believe that God is working something great inside of you for His glory.

Job was taken by storm when the reports came that he had lost his children, his house, and his livestock. Then, on top of these serial tragedies, extreme and sudden sickness overcame his body. But why? Job walked upright before God.
Why?

Job was volunteered by God to endure great suffering and loss because God wanted to show the enemy Job's faith. God wanted to show the enemy Job's endurance. Finally, God wanted to show the enemy that Job would not forsake Him. Although, at one point Job said, "Though You may slay me, I will trust You," yet in another trying moment, Job was cursing the day he was born, his statements and his actions in the face of his fiery trials demonstrate that while Job experienced times of great strength and times of feeling as if death would be better than living, that he still stood strong in His faith regardless. Job persevered and received double of everything that he had lost and so will you.

Do not give up. Stay strong in the faith!

LIFE Meditation

Devotion 6

Stay Strong in the Faith

Let's Meditate on Job 1:13-22

Now there was a day when his sons and daughters were eating and drinking wine in their oldest brother's house; and a messenger came to Job and said, "The oxen were plowing and the donkeys feeding beside them, when the Sabeans raided them and took them away – indeed they have killed the servants with the edge of the sword; and I alone have escaped to tell you!" While he was still speaking, another also came and said, "The fire of God fell from heaven and burned up the sheep and the servants and consumed them; and I alone have escaped to tell you!" While he was still speaking, another also came and said, "The Chaldeans formed three bands, raided the camels and took them away, yes, and killed the servants with the edge of the sword; and I alone have escaped to tell you!" While he was still speaking, another also came and said, "Your sons and daughters were eating and drinking wine in their oldest brother's house, and suddenly a great wind came from across the wilderness and struck the four corners of the house, and it fell on the young people, and they are dead; and I alone have escaped to tell you!" Then Job arose, tore his robe, and shaved his head; and he fell to the ground and worshiped. And he said: "Naked I came from my mother's womb, and naked shall I return there. The Lord gave, and the Lord has taken away; blessed be the name of the Lord." In all this Job did not sin nor charge God with wrong.

❃

What do you hear God saying to you today? So that you can remember, let's write what you are thinking and feeling down right now.

_____

_____

_____

_____

_____

_____

_____

_____

_____

_____

_____

_____

_____

_____

_____

_____

_____

Be Everything That You Were Called to Be

Devotion 7

MUHSIN THORNTON

Be Everything That You Were Called to Be

Once, while some Israelites were burying a man, suddenly they saw a band of raiders; so, they threw the man's body into Elisha's tomb. When the body touched Elisha's bones, the man came to life and stood up on his feet.

2 Kings 13:21 21

✄

While my wife and I were in Costa Rica, we had a tour guide name Marco. Marco taught us about sugar cane. Sugar cane is Costa Rica's most plentiful resource and it has many uses. The cane is used to produce white sugar, brown sugar, and molasses. Costa Ricans even burn the sugarcane to make fuel. The more I learned about the nature of sugar cane, the more I began to think, "Man I want to be useful for many purposes -- I want to be like sugarcane."

Whatever God has intended to use me to accomplish for Him, that is what I want to do.

When Marco told us that sugarcane ash is used for fertilizer, I really got excited. Not only does the cane serve multiple, very important functions that help people every single day, but the sugar cane serves and helps the people even after it is burned and buried. When I die, I want my legacy to live on and to infinitely impact lives just like Costa Rican sugar cane.

Except for Jesus, the prophet Elisha had the most recorded miracles in the Bible and like Jesus, and sugar cane, Elisha was extraordinarily impactful even from the grave. According to 2 Kings 13:21, the Israelites threw a dead man's body into Elisha tomb and miraculously, when the dead man's body touched the prophet Elisha's bones, the man came to life and stood up on his feet.

Let's decide to be useful today, both in life and in death. Let's decide to be everything that God called us to be.

LIFE Meditation

Devotion 7

Be Everything That You Were Called to Be

Let's Meditate on 2 Kings 13:21 21

Once while some Israelites were burying a man, suddenly they saw a band of raiders; so, they threw the man's body into Elisha's tomb. When the body touched Elisha's bones, the man came to life and stood up on his feet.

What do you hear God saying to you today? So that you can remember, let's write what you are thinking and feeling down right now.

Nothing but Good Vibes

Devotion 8

MUHSIN THORNTON

Nothing but Good Vibes

The LORD has done it this very day; let us rejoice today and be glad.

Psalm 118:24

Do not boast about tomorrow, for you do not know what a day may bring.

Proverb 27:1

Tomorrow is not promised to you. Actually, the next minute is not even promised to you. Don't live your life with regrets. If you want to do something, get organized, get up and do it. Just do it. Do it today.

Life is way too short to say I'll do it tomorrow. Tomorrow may never come. Life is too short to be bitter, and to hold grudges or to give off negative vibes. Exude positivity no matter what the situation is. This is the day the Lord has made, and we should rejoice and be glad in it. Let's rejoice about our second chances, about the gifts, hopes and dreams that God put in our hearts, and about the fact that we were blessed to live another day -- somebody didn't make it through last night.

Embrace every single moment of today. While you are out and about, look for ways to share nothing but your good vibes!

LIFE Meditation

Devotion 8

Nothing but Good Vibes

Let's Meditate on Psalm 118:24 and Proverbs 27:1

The LORD has done it this very day; let us rejoice today and be glad.

Psalm 118:24

Do not boast about tomorrow, for you do not know what a day may bring.

Proverbs 27:1

✖

What do you hear God saying to you today? So that you can remember, let's write what you are thinking and feeling down right now.

_____

_____

_____

_____

_____

_____

_____

Don't Let Them Tear You Up

Devotion 9

MUHSIN THORNTON

Don't Let Them Tear You Up

Be sober, be vigilant; because your adversary the devil, as a roaring lion, walks about, seeking whom he may devour.

1 Peter 5:8

❀

The enemy wants to devour you today, but don't you dare allow him to tear you up. I'm reminded of a show I used to watch called *American Gladiators*. My favorite competition was called the Powerball. During this challenge, contenders attempted to score by depositing colored balls into narrow cylinders while simultaneously trying to evade the three Gladiators who defended the playing field. Every time the contender would try to get that ball into the cylinder, the Gladiator would rush towards them and mercilessly toss them around. I'd yell, "Oh my goodness, that Gladiator just tore them up!"

The ball that the contenders carry in their attempt to get the ball into the cylinder represents your happiness, your joy, and your peace. That cylinder is your day and that Gladiator -- that's satan -- he is your enemy.

The enemy tries to take the happiness, joy and peace out of your day. I remember the contenders used to try to bob and weave to get to the cylinder. That seemed logical to me at one point in my life but knowing what I know now about the authority God has given to you and to me, I recommend that you advance in full force directly toward your enemy.

Your most powerful strategy when it comes to defeating your enemy is prayer. Just pray. Don't allow anyone to take your happiness, joy, or peace today. Your Gladiator can come in the form of your boss, your co-worker, or the guy riding beside you on your way to work. It may be your spouse, your children or a friend you love dearly. It could be health, finances, or some other very difficult circumstance. Whatever it is, don't let them tear you up.

LIFE Meditation

Devotion 9

Don't Let Them Tear You Up

Let's Meditate on 1 Peter 5:8

Be sober, be vigilant; because your adversary the devil, as a roaring lion, walks about, seeking whom he may devour.

What do you hear God saying to you today? So that you can remember, let's write what you are thinking and feeling down right now.

Be a Multiplier

Devotion 10

Be a Multiplier

And God blessed them, and God said unto them, be fruitful, and multiply.

Genesis 1:28

I wisdom dwell with prudence and find out knowledge of witty inventions.
Proverbs 8:12

❧

You *must* call yourself a multiplier. God told you to be fruitful and multiply and that does not only mean go out and have babies. What God means is that whenever you put your hands to a task, a community, a person's life, or to anything, that increase should occur.

You are supposed to add to people lives and are never to subtract from their lives. You are to bring positivity. You are not to be the bearer of bad news. You are responsible and equipped to elevate and motivate people. In every situation, you were created to be productive. You were created to bring forth new ideas, or what the Bible calls, witty inventions. Your assignment is to produce nothing less than double what you receive.

You are an asset and not a liability. You are a multiplier.

LIFE Meditation

Devotion 10

Be a Multiplier

Let's Meditate on Genesis 1:28 and Proverb 8:12.

And God blessed them, and God said unto them, Be fruitful, and multiply,

Genesis 1:28

I wisdom dwell with prudence and find out knowledge of witty inventions.

Proverbs 8:12

❧

What do you hear God saying to you today? So that you can remember, let's write what you are thinking and feeling down right now.

_____

_____

_____

It is What You Say It Is

Devotion 11

It is What You Say It Is

The thief cometh not, but for to steal, and to kill, and to destroy: I am come that they might have life, and that they might have it more abundantly.

John 10:10

Death and life are in the power of the tongue: and they that love it shall eat the fruit thereof.

Proverbs 18:21

❧

Let's not settle for less today. What do I mean? Let's not use the popular phrase, "It is what it is". It is not what it is. It is what you say it is! You can't speak negativity over your job, over your marriage, and over your children's life and expect to witness miracles. You can't throw up your hands and accept anything less than what God promised you -- and He promised you a life of abundance (John 10:10). Instead, watch how you speak, for there is life and death in the power of the tongue (Proverbs 18:21).

You speak things into existence when you talk. If you say something enough, it will eventually take root and manifest. First you think it, then you say it, then you become it. So, stop and think about what you want from life and what you want to be before you SPEAK. It is not just what it is -- it is what you say it is.

LIFE Meditation

Devotion 11

It Is What You Say It Is

Let's Meditate on John 10:10 and Proverbs 18:21

The thief cometh not, but for to steal, and to kill, and to destroy: I am come that they might have life, and that they might have it more abundantly.

John 10:10

Death and life are in the power of the tongue: and they that love it shall eat the fruit thereof.

Proverbs 18:21

What do you hear God saying to you today? So that you can remember, let's write what you are thinking and feeling down right now.

Stick to Your Assignment

Devotion 12

MUHSIN THORNTON

Stick to Your Assignment

Then the sailors said to each other, "Come, let us cast lots to find out who is responsible for this calamity." They cast lots and the lot fell on Jonah. So, they asked him, "Tell us, who is responsible for making all this trouble for us? What kind of work do you do? Where do you come from? What is your country? From what people are you?" He answered, "I am a Hebrew and I worship the Lord, the God of heaven, who made the sea and the dry land." This terrified them, and they asked, "What have you done?" (They knew he was running away from the Lord, because he had already told them so.)

Jonah 1:7-10

❧

STay on your assignment. When you go off task you start wasting time. When you go against God's will, you don't only affect your life, you affect the lives of the people connected to and influenced by you.

The Bible speaks about a man named Jonah. God told Jonah to go to one place, but Jonah decided to go somewhere else (Jonah 1). Jonah was off-task and his decision to disobey God's instruction caused a great storm to occur.

Are you causing the storms in your life by being disobedient to the call of God? You could be much farther than you are if you would just listen. Right now, you might be on a job that's not related to your assignment and you may feel that you are just wasting time, or you might be at the exact place where God put you. If you are in position already, stick to your assignment. If you are off course, quickly make the adjustment, and then stick to your assignment.

In the movie "The Jungle Book" the boy Mobley was raised by wolves. In time, it became dangerous for Mobley to exist with the wolves. The tiger came after him and destroyed everything in his path to get to Mobley. Mobley felt pressured to go back to mankind, so the tiger would stop his destructive ways, but Mobley stayed. Mobley stayed and finished his assignment. Mobley was the only one who could defeat the tiger, it was crucial that he stayed on task. Similarly, you are the only one who can finish your assignment. It is crucial that you stay on task. Your life is not the only life that depends on it.

LIFE Meditation

Devotion 12

Stick to Your Assignment

Let's Meditate on Jonah 1:7-10

Then the sailors said to each other, "Come, let us cast lots to find out who is responsible for this calamity." They cast lots and the lot fell on Jonah. 8 So they asked him, "Tell us, who is responsible for making all this trouble for us? What kind of work do you do? Where do you come from? What is your country? From what people are you?" He answered, "I am a Hebrew and I worship the Lord, the God of heaven, who made the sea and the dry land." This terrified them, and they asked, "What have you done?" (They knew he was running away from the Lord, because he had already told them so.)

❅

What do you hear God saying to you today? So that you can remember, let's write what you are thinking and feeling down right now.

Champions Adjust

Devotion 13

MUHSIN THORNTON

Champions Adjust

So, Abram said to Lot, "Let's not have any quarreling between you and me, or between your herders and mine, for we are close relatives. Is not the whole land before you? Let's part company. If you go to the left, I'll go to the right; if you go to the right, I'll go to the left." Lot looked around and saw that the whole plain of the Jordan toward Zoar was well watered, like the garden of the Lord, like the land of Egypt. (This was before the Lord destroyed Sodom and Gomorrah.) So, Lot chose for himself the whole plain of the Jordan and set out toward the east. The two men parted company: Abram lived in the land of Canaan, while Lot lived among the cities of the plain and pitched his tents near Sodom.

Genesis 13:8-12

❧

The differences between becoming a champion and finishing in second place is a matter of making the necessary adjustments. I can remember going into one of my championship games. I had a strategy of pitching my changeup pitcher first and then I'd use my fastball pitcher, but, in that game, my opponent was ready for me and I did not expect that. Once the manager on the other team found out how my pitcher was pitching, he told his team to sit on the pitches. They ended up beating my team the first two innings, which made me switch pitchers sooner than I had planned. All I could do is pray that my second guy would hold up, but that day, my prayers were not answered. We lost that championship because I didn't make the necessary adjustments to be a champion that day.

Life will throw you curveballs. You must quickly adjust and refuse to allow unexpected challenges and changes to rattle you. Just take a deep breathe, relax your mind, and make the necessary changes.

The adjustment may be minor but making the right adjustments can lead to tremendous wins. Do you need to adjust your schedule, your attitude, your jump shot, your swing, your work technique, or your relationships?

Abraham had to adjust his living arrangements with his nephew Lot because their herdsmen were at strife (Genesis 13-14). For Abraham to win he had to make a quick adjustment because, like Jay-Z said, "Nobody wins when the family feuds". Abraham had a conversation with Lot. He basically told him, "I'll take the land that you don't want". It looked as if Lot took the better of the land, but Abraham got the best land out of the deal. God rewarded Abraham because Abram made the adjustment.

You are a champion. Make the adjustment.

LIFE Meditation

Devotion 13

Champions Adjust

Let's Meditate on Genesis 13:8-12

So, Abram said to Lot, "Let's not have any quarreling between you and me, or between your herders and mine, for we are close relatives. Is not the whole land before you? Let's part company. If you go to the left, I'll go to the right; if you go to the right, I'll go to the left." Lot looked around and saw that the whole plain of the Jordan toward Zoar was well watered, like the garden of the Lord, like the land of Egypt. (This was before the Lord destroyed Sodom and Gomorrah.) So, Lot chose for himself the whole plain of the Jordan and set out toward the east. The two men parted company: Abram lived in the land of Canaan, while Lot lived among the cities of the plain and pitched his tents near Sodom.

Genesis 13:8-12

❋

What do you hear God saying to you today? So that
you can remember, let's write what you are thinking
and feeling down right now.

_____

_____

_____

_____

_____

_____

_____

_____

_____

_____

_____

_____

_____

_____

_____

_____

_____

_____

_____

_____

MUHSIN THORNTON

Stay in Your Lane

Devotion 14

Stay in Your Lane

You shall not covet your neighbor's house; you shall not covet your neighbor's wife or his male servant or his female servant or his ox or his donkey or anything that belongs to your neighbor.

Exodus 20:17

To everything there is a season, and a time to every purpose under the heaven.

Ecclesiastes 3:1

❧

You can't do everything that everybody else is doing. You can't measure your success by what the next man is doing. Just because somebody is moving and having success faster than you are, does not mean your winning season is not a couple of years or, even better, a few months or days away.

The problem is that when things don't happen fast enough, instead of staying in our own lane, we switch lanes then wonder, "Why don't things feel right?" Things don't feel right for you because you are not in your lane. It's not the field that you are called to be in. It's not the class that you should be taking. You can't be out here trying to buy and flip houses if your bank account can't handle it, or even more importantly, if God has called you to work to fulfill His will and bring His name glory by doing some other type of work. Life is, in this example, like driving -- getting in a lane that you do not belong in usually ends up in an accident.

Just do what you do, your time of supernatural overflow is coming.

LIFE Meditation

Devotion 14

Stay in Your Lane

Let's Meditate on Exodus 20:17 and Ecclesiastes 3:1

You shall not covet your neighbor's house; you shall not covet your neighbor's wife or his male servant or his female servant or his ox or his donkey or anything that belongs to your neighbor.

Exodus 20:17

To everything there is a season, and a time to every purpose under the heaven.

Ecclesiastes 3:1

❊

What do you hear God saying to you today? So that you can remember, let's write what you are thinking and feeling down right now.

Don't Be So Emotional

Devotion 15

Don't Be So Emotional

One evening David got up from his bed and walked around on the roof of the palace. From the roof he saw a woman bathing. The woman was very beautiful, and David sent someone to find out about her. The man said, "She is Bathsheba, the daughter of Eliam and the wife of Uriah the Hittite." Then David sent messengers to get her. She came to him, and he slept with her.

2 Samuel 11:2-4, 14-15

✖

Don't make emotional decisions today. Emotional decisions lead to lifelong regrets. Proverbs 4:23 says, "Out of the heart flows the issues of life." So, it's not unnatural for you to just react without thinking it through or for you to react based on how you feel. We all have moments when we react without weighing the pros and cons.

In the story of David and Bathsheba (2 Samuel 11). David spots Bathsheba on the rooftop and lusts after her. There was one problem. Bathsheba was married to Uriah. David made two decisions based on what he was feeling. First, he slept with a married woman. Second, to cover up his sin, he orchestrated Uriah's death. David's decisions lead to Bathsheba having a stillbirth child. There are always consequences for the decisions we make. So, as you make decisions, large and small today, weigh it out, pray it out, and then decide. But whatever you do, do not make a hasty, emotional decision.

LIFE Meditation

Devotion 15

Don't Be So Emotional

Let's Meditate on 2 Samuel 11:2-4, 14-15

One evening David got up from his bed and walked around on the roof of the palace. From the roof he saw a woman bathing. The woman was very beautiful, and David sent someone to find out about her. The man said, "She is Bathsheba, the daughter of Eliam and the wife of Uriah the Hittite." Then David sent messengers to get her. She came to him, and he slept with her.

�֍

What do you hear God saying to you today? So that you can remember, let's write what you are thinking and feeling down right now.

_____

_____

_____

_____

_____

Everybody Can't Go with You

Devotion 16

Everybody Can't Go with You

When Jesus entered the synagogue leader's house and saw the noisy crowd and people playing pipes, he said, "Go away. The girl is not dead but asleep." But they laughed at him. After the crowd had been put outside, he went in and took the girl by the hand, and she got up. News of this spread through all that region.

Matthew 9:23-26

❀

When you're trying to go to the next level in life and in business, you can't take everybody with you. Jesus fed five thousand, appointed seventy-two disciples, and hand-selected twelve disciples. When it was time to go to the Mount of Transformation He took three of the twelve disciples with Him. When it was time to go into the house to raise the little girl from the dead, He took three disciples with Him. When it was time to go into the Garden of Gethsemane, He took three disciples with him. He took James, John, and Peter with him at crucial times in his ministry. They were ready for the next level.

You can't take people with you who are not ready. They'll end up slowing you down. If you're serious about going to the next level, you better look at the company you keep and start disassociating yourself with the people who are not prepared to go to the next level with you. Find out where their hearts are and know their mindset. Where God is taking you requires people that can handle the pressure, handle the criticism, and handle the uncomfortable.

Everybody can't go!

If you have been wondering why you can't seem to reach your peak, it may be because you have surrounded yourself with the wrong company. It's time for you to go into that house to bring new life to dead situations. It's time for you to enter new depths of prayer, suffering, and success with loyal people. You've fed the masses, you've mentored and helped people grow, now it's time to release some folk. You're moving on up.

LIFE Meditation

Devotion 16

Everybody Can't Go with You

Let's Meditate on Matthew 9:23-26

When Jesus entered the synagogue leader's house and saw the noisy crowd and people playing pipes, he said, "Go away. The girl is not dead but asleep." But they laughed at him. After the crowd had been put outside, he went in and took the girl by the hand, and she got up. News of this spread through all that region.

✺

What do you hear God saying to you today? So that you can remember, let's write what you are thinking and feeling down right now.

_____

_____

_____

_____

_____

Own It

Devotion 17

MUHSIN THORNTON

Own It

God said to the man, "Who told you that you were naked? Did you eat fruit from that special tree? I told you not to eat from that tree!" The man said, "The woman you put here with me gave me fruit from that tree. So, I ate it."

Genesis 3:11-12

❈

It never surprises me when people don't take accountability for their own actions. People don't take accountability for where they are in life. You cannot go around blaming other people, your childhood, or anything else for what you have or have not accomplished in life. Whether you grew up with both of your parents, in a single parent home, or in foster care, none of these are the reason for why you have not excelled at this point in your life.

Responsibility and accountability have been important character traits since the beginning of time. God asked Adam a question and Adam replied that,

"It was the woman that you gave me. She made me do this." Wow! Not only did Adam blame Eve for his decision, Adam blamed God too.

Listen, it is too late in the game to point fingers at people for your mistakes. It's time to stand up and be a man or a woman enough about it -- whatever *it* is for you. I have decided that if I am not where I want to be in life, that it is because of me. Am I procrastinating? Am I being lazy? Am I scared? Whatever the reason it is, I don't care, but I look no further than the man in the mirror and when our eyes meet, I look dead at him and say, "Own It, Muh!"

Today, I pray that you will too.

LIFE Meditation

Devotion 17

Own it

Let's Meditate on Genesis 3:11-12

God said to the man, "Who told you that you were naked? Did you eat fruit from that special tree? I told you not to eat from that tree!" The man said, "The woman you put here with me gave me fruit from that tree. So, I ate it."

✄

What do you hear God saying to you today? So that you can remember, let's write what you are thinking and feeling down right now.

_____

_____

_____

_____

_____

_____

Full Throttle

Devotion 18

Full Throttle

*Then Samuel said to Jesse, "Are all your sons here?"
And he said, "There remains yet the youngest, but
behold, he is keeping the sheep." And Samuel said to
Jesse, "Send and get him, for we will not sit down till
he comes here." And he sent and brought him in. Now
he was ruddy and had beautiful eyes and was
handsome. And the Lord said, "Arise, anoint him, for
this is he." Then Samuel took the horn of oil and
anointed him in the midst of his brothers. And the
Spirit of the Lord rushed upon David from that day
forward. And Samuel rose up and went to Ramah.*

1 Samuel 16:11-13

❦

Whatever you do, whatever line of business that you are in, you must go hard. You can't afford to take a play off. I used to play high school football. I wasn't the greatest player in the world, but I played against some pretty good players. In fact, these players were Division I recruits, so every time they played, scouts would come out watch them and every time I played against one of them, I played especially hard. I would go full throttle because I knew that scouts were watching. Going full throttle means giving whatever the task at hand is your absolute best. I do everything full throttle because I never know who might be watching me. Think about it, they might like how you dance, like how you sing, like how you work the office, or love the way you engage an audience when you speak. You don't know what opportunity may present itself, so I go hard.

I'm sure that when David was anointed king, he wasn't surprised. David knew that he protected his father's sheep as best he could -- he shepherded on full throttle. He killed the lion and the bear, and he was ready to handle being a king. Don't let anything catch you by surprise today. Someone is looking to discover, bless and promote you. Be ready. Go harder than you ever have before. Today is your day!

LIFE Meditation

Devotional 18

Full Throttle

Let's Meditate on 1 Samuel 16:11-13

Then Samuel said to Jesse, "Are all your sons here?" And he said, "There remains yet the youngest, but behold, he is keeping the sheep." And Samuel said to Jesse, "Send and get him, for we will not sit down till he comes here." And he sent and brought him in. Now he was ruddy and had beautiful eyes and was handsome. And the Lord said, "Arise, anoint him, for this is he." Then Samuel took the horn of oil and anointed him in the midst of his brothers. And the Spirit of the Lord rushed upon David from that day forward. And Samuel rose up and went to Ramah.

❈

What do you hear God saying to you today? So that you can remember, let's write what you are thinking and feeling down right now.

_____

_____

Just Win

Devotion 19

MUHSIN THORNTON

Just Win

For God hath not given us the spirit of fear, but of power and of love and of a sound mind.

2 Timothy 1:7

But Jesus looked at them and said to them, "With men this is impossible, but with God all things are possible."

Matthew 19:26

❧

God didn't give you a spirit of fear, but of joy, peace, and a sound mind. Just go out and win. The only thing stopping you from winning is yourself. Your lack of determination is stopping you. Your lack of drive is stopping you. Your lack of commitment is stopping you. Your lack of passion is stopping you. Your fear is stopping you.

Why do you keep waiting for tomorrow? Tomorrow may never come. It's time to win now.

It's the fourth quarter. Ten seconds are left on the clock and you've got the ball. Only you can stop you in this moment. Remember that you were created to win. You were created to succeed. Losing is never an option. No matter how the circumstances look, you will win.

Greater is He that is in you, than he that is in the world.

All you do is WIN! Go be victorious today.

LIFE Meditation

Devotional 19

Just Win

Let's Meditate on 2 Timothy 1:7 and Matthew 19:26

For God hath not given us the spirit of fear, but of power and of love and of a sound mind.

2 Timothy 1:7

But Jesus looked at them and said to them, "With men this is impossible, but with God all things are possible."

Matthew 19:26

�֎

What do you hear God saying to you today? So that you can remember, let's write what you are thinking and feeling down right now.

_____

_____

_____

Take the Necessary Steps

Devotion 20

Take the Necessary Steps

To everything there is a season, and a time to every purpose under the heaven.

Ecclesiastes 3:1

We must respect the fact that everything requires a process. We can't just can't skip steps. It is in the process of trying to accomplish something, that we learn invaluable lessons and have important experiences at each phase. The challenge is that we live in a "microwave society". We want everything right now, but patience is a virtue.

At times I wonder if the prodigal son had been given his inheritance over time, instead of all at once, how his life would have been different. Perhaps he'd have valued a dollar more and would not have just not spent his money frivolously.

Elisha had to be mentored by Elijah and he did not receive Elijah's mantle until the prophet was taken up. Elisha went through the process of serving, learning from and walking with his mentor and, because of his patience with the process, Elisha was blessed with a double portion of Elijah's incredible anointing -- he waited -- and he ended up performing twice the miracles of his teacher because of it.

LIFE Meditation

Devotional 20

Take the Necessary Steps

Let's Meditate on Ecclesiastes 3:1

To everything there is a season, and a time to every purpose under the heaven.

�֍

What do you hear God saying to you today? So that you can remember, let's write what you are thinking and feeling down right now.

_____

_____

_____

_____

_____

_____

_____

_____

_____

_____

_____
_____
_____
_____
_____
_____
_____
_____
_____
_____
_____
_____
_____
_____
_____
_____
_____
_____
_____
_____
_____
_____
_____
_____
_____
_____
_____
_____

Stay Humble

Devotion 21

Stay Humble

Then Moses went up from the plains of Moab to Mount Nebo, to the top of Pisgah, which is across from Jericho. And the Lord showed him all the land of Gilead as far as Dan, all Naphtali and the land of Ephraim and Manasseh, all the land of Judah as far as the Western Sea, the South, and the plain of the Valley of Jericho, the city of palm trees, as far as Zoar. Then the Lord said to him, "This is the land of which I swore to give Abraham, Isaac, and Jacob, saying, 'I will give it to your descendants.' I have caused you to see it with your eyes, but you shall not cross over there."

Deuteronomy 34:1-4

❦

God has you on the brink of something awesome. I mean pure greatness is in you, and because of this, it is very important for you to remain humble.

For 20 days you been positive. You are encouraged, and the promises of God are on their way to you. Let's not forget where your strength comes from. Moses got caught up in himself. In Numbers 20, God told Moses to speak to the rock so that water would flow out of the rock for the people. Instead, Moses struck the rock with his staff. This act cost Moses the opportunity to walk into the promise land because Moses' act of selfishness made the people look to him, instead of at God as the performer of miracles.

God is the creator of all and the doer of all. Not only did Moses disobey God, but he looked down on the people. The minute we forget about where we came from or that God delivered you from some unspeakable things too, is the minute we fall. Remember, pride comes before the fall.

The blessings and increase are going to begin to overflow for you today. Remain humble and remember to always tell everyone who compliments you, that all you have and all you have become, is because of God.

LIFE Meditation

Devotional 21

Stay Humble

Let's Meditate on Deuteronomy 34:1-4

Then Moses went up from the plains of Moab to Mount Nebo, to the top of Pisgah, which is across from Jericho. And the Lord showed him all the land of Gilead as far as Dan, all Naphtali and the land of Ephraim and Manasseh, all the land of Judah as far as the Western Sea, the South, and the plain of the Valley of Jericho, the city of palm trees, as far as Zoar. Then the Lord said to him, "This is the land of which I swore to give Abraham, Isaac, and Jacob, saying, 'I will give it to your descendants.' I have caused you to see it with your eyes, but you shall not cross over there."

What do you hear God saying to you today? So that you can remember, let's write what you are thinking and feeling down right now.

About the Author

Muhsin Isheem Thornton, Sr. was born in Philadelphia, Pennsylvania to Bryan Thornton, II and Angela Dyson. At the age of eighteen Muhsin decided to leave Philadelphia and relocate to Willingboro, New Jersey. It was there, in New Jersey, at Macedonia Baptist Church, where he gave his life to Christ. Shortly afterwards Muhsin started leading worship service and was appointed as a walking deacon.

Eventually, Muhsin became a member of New Direction Church under the leadership of Pastor Lawrence Forman. There, under the tutelage of Apostle Bernice Jackson, he learned how to operate in the Holy Spirit. Two years later, Muhsin was ordained as a minister and after finishing Bible classes he became Youth Pastor at New Direction Church.

Thornton also studied at Open Hand Evangelistic School and Trinity College of Bible and Theological Seminary. In April of 2009, Muhsin was ordained as an elder in the house of the lord by Bishop William Young, Jr. Called by the Lord in 2010, and with the guidance of Bishop William Young, Jr., Muhsin and Elder Lawrence Foreman, Jr., co-founded New Birth Deliverance Temple in Willingboro, New Jersey. Muhsin served as the Assistant Pastor of New Birth.

Today he worships and serves at Higher Ground International under the leadership of Pastors Steven and Wanda Martin. Minister Muhsin teaches the word of God, preaches the word of God, and serves as Director of the Sound Department.

Muhsin is also the Founder and Executive Director of *We Are*, a mentoring program based in Philadelphia, Pennsylvania. Using the LIFE leadership model, the mission of *We Are* is to empower young men ages 11-15, who live in the inner city, to love themselves and to live their best lives.

Finally, be strong in the Lord and in his mighty power.

Ephesians 6:10

www.ingramcontent.com/pod-product-compliance
Lightning Source LLC
LaVergne TN
LVHW021501080426
835509LV00018B/2362